On the Line
A Collection of prose and poetry by
members of The University of East Anglia's
Creative Writing Society

Anthology 2021

Creative Writing Society

On the Line
First published by Egg Box Publishing 2021

Part of UEA Publishing Project, Ltd.
International ©2021 retained by individual authors
A CIP record for this book is available at the British Library

This book is sold subject to the condition that it shall not, by way of trade or otherwise, be lent, resold, hired out, stored in a retrieval system, or otherwise circulated without the publisher's prior consent in any form of binding or cover other than that in which it is published and without a similar condition including this condition being imposed on the subsequent purchaser.
Squeeze is typeset in Times New Roman Bold
Titles are set in Times New Roman Regular
Designed and typeset by Mackenzie Malcolm
Printed and bound in the UK by Imprint Digital
Distributed by Inpress
ISBN 978-1-913861-21-6 >>

The Editorial Team

EDITOR-IN-CHIEF   Clara Ehlers & Silas Hand

EDITORIAL BOARD   Alex Grenfell
Anna Rumsby
Elif Soyler
Siobhan Horner
Emma Asshetton-Smith
Sophie Rose-Land
Mackenzie Malcolm
Biff Pearson
Erin Ketteridge
Alex Eaglestone

COVER DESIGN   Meg Watts

INTERIOR ILLUSTRATIONS   Liz Lane

TYPESETTING   Mackenzie Malcolm

CONTENTS

Chapter 1

The Nymph	Clem Hailes	9
Iridescent Birds	Barnaby Hill	11
You and You and You	Basita	13
Delicious Bugs		14
Never Mind!		15
Late Summer/Early Autumn	Biff Pearson	16
Cuttings	Denise Monroe	18
Snakeskin	Jessica Lily Blissitt	20
Round Eyes	Kiera Stibbons	21
the waterfall	Lucy Cundill	24
Seasons Change	Max Wrigley	26
Love and a Can of Worms	Samuel Glyn	27
Advert for the Latest Apocalypse	Seb Gale	29
What Can You Say?	Silas Hand	30

Chapter 2

The Fool	Clem Hailes	33
Love Letter	Alex Eaglestone	35
Astrid and Askeladden	Anna Rumsby	37
How to Love I & II	Clara Ehlers	40
East London, June, 2016	Elif Soyler	42
My Sky is Not Blue	Emma Bullen	44
Mini Smarties	Erin Ketteridge	46
Mum's Favourite Game	Jess Miller	48
Not Me	Oihane Garcia	50
Oystercatcher	Oliver Shrouder	51
Electric Razor		52
Storytime	Ray Khawaja	53
Evelyn: Extract from a Novel	Shannon Clinton-Copeland	55

Chapter 3

The Bard	*Clem Hailes*	59
Smoke	*Alec Goldstone*	61
Foreign Land - A Journal Entry	*David Davies*	65
Freddie Starr Ate My Hampster	*Elif Soyler*	67
Stutter	*Jessica Lily Blissitt*	69
Three Letters in a Pandemic	*Liz Lane*	70
A Vaccine for Father Christmas	*Madeline Donnelly*	75
Mama Meant Well	*Sam Gordon-Webb*	78
An Email	*Silas Hand*	80

Chapter 4

The Knight	*Clem Hailes*	83
Kristna at Auschwitz	*Alex Grenfell*	87
I Want	*Eleanor Burleigh*	90
Generation Y	*Ellen Newall*	92
Robin	*Eve O'Donoghue*	94
Let Me Go	*Lilwen-Meyer Dinkgrafe*	96
Ghost	*Meg Watts*	99
Ten Easy Steps to Build Confidence	*Rose Ramsden*	100

Creative Writing Society

Introduction

It goes without saying that this has been a very strange year, but as we reach its end, we hope you enjoy this sample of all the fantastic work that Creative Writing Society members have produced. Throughout this year we have continued to meet online, with fantastic open-mics, workshops and crit groups, which we hope have brought you all together in some way. And, as we look forward to a (hopefully) more normal future, we hope you use this book to look back on some of the better memories of a, quite frankly, crap time.

So, we'd like to welcome you to this year's anthology, featuring amazing poetry, prose and everything in between, with fantastic illustrations by Liz Lane and cover design by Meg Watts. Sit back, grab a cup of tea (or a glass of wine) and settle in to *On the Line*...

Creative Writing Society

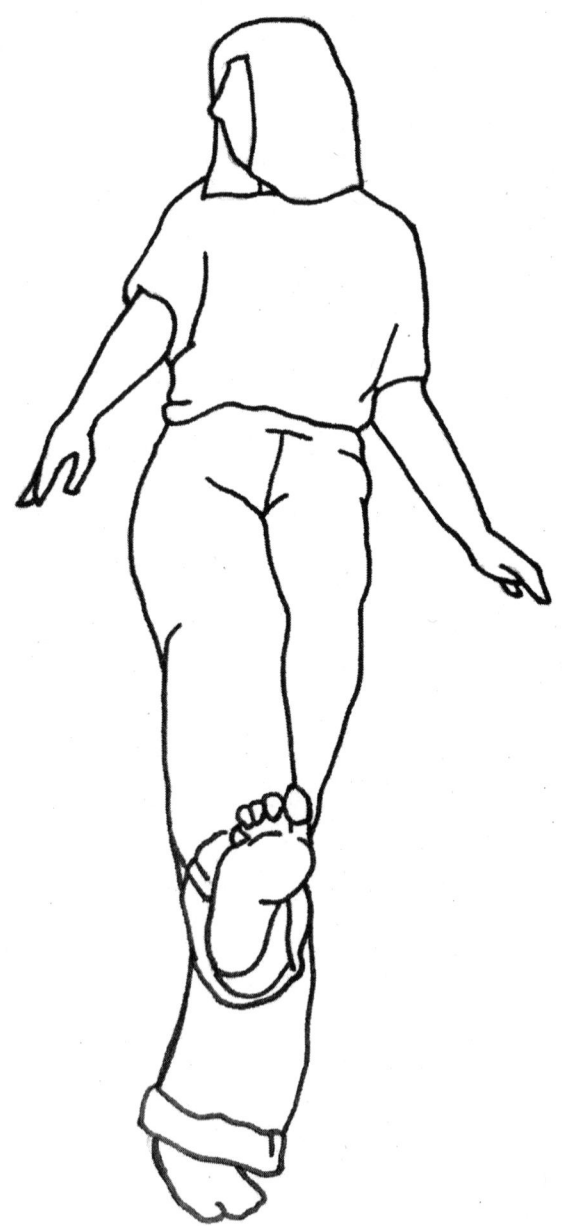

Chapter 1

The Nymph

I wished on a log
Heart hopeful and limbs oaken
Moss cradling my cheek

Wild roses crave water
Petals shimmering with pearls
Roots soaked and sated

Water's edge. Cool, damp
I like that. Old wood is warm
But grass is soft too

Your mind holds treasure
Mine is fool's gold swathed in leaves
Lucky I love fools

Clem Hailes

Creative Writing Society

Iridescent Birds

he feeds her a line, like honey,
dripping between the gaps in his teeth.
and when he's gone,
she spits it out,
from the back of her mouth,
repulsed by the flavour of
                syrup on catshit;
as though the abyss
of her head was a cesspit.
while he runs wild
and keeps her shrouded in the undergrowth,
like the flare of his Lover
doesn't burn brighter in the shadows.

he doesn't know
she's living on those lines,
crouched beneath the covers,
face blue in the phone light,
repeating them, to his Lover,
words trickling off her tongue

growing sweeter;
he's paranoid
she found the Polaroids
                in the lining of his coat,
Their skin as succulent as midnight rain.

she ferments her hatred
until it crackles in her throat
like the thrum of the love he lost
until there is nothing left of him inside,
so she upheaves herself,
loses herself,
in Them.
he's working late again.

lost into the soft susurration of silence.
she feels cool palms
lie against the small of her back
dew droplets hover, wet, on their green curves,
she craves to quench her masochism
over the soothing glisten of Their beauty.

and she dreams
of tall ferns and fronds
obscuring the lover's naked breast
while she kisses Them
for the salvation from her nothingness.
and she begins to taste the lines of honey
that dart overhead
like the journey of iridescent birds.

Barnaby Hill

You and You and You

Sorry! I have a calling
do you know
we all have a soul
and it calls out
Oh, you don't?
How would you!
Aren't you busy?
in looking at my clothes
or
thinking how you should 'act'
in families, societies or
even when alone.
well, I have a soul
it speaks so loudly
that it deafens me
I can't hear you
and you and you all.

Basita

Delicious Bugs

They call me sweet ugly
sharp and dangerous
I have it in my aura
fingers pointing towards me
I am guilty
yes! in your court
I am guilty
I don't plead
plead in front of frogs
quaking in the pond?
I have known myself
I seek myself
not the pond
the mud
the leaves
I seek myself.
Who are you?
Say 'Quack'.

Basita

Never Mind!

Why this and not that,
another feather? bring my hat!
Rush, rush!! wait, left or right
just one last look at my map
bring me tea, no sugary drink
but extra cheese on my burger I think!
Hello old friend, I missed you so
what's your name? forget it though!
My lover got such beautiful eyes
how dare he blink more than twice?
I want to fight and tear him apart
just one mistake, then eat his heart!
I crack a joke, you have to laugh
fake it, make it, I'll split in half.
Oh, my friends, you're all damned!
but can I kiss you, beforehand?
Being a bitch and also a clown
has turned my world upside down!
Romeo, Romeo! Where have you been?
My glass slipper, has anyone seen?
Before you could reach me through my long hair
I ate snow white's poisonous pear
No, not pear but I had to rhyme
I lost it here, never mind!

Basita

Late Summer/Early Autumn

Buddleia, heavy set your roots.
Midnight flower bloom in green parcel;
draw light from soil, draw dark from bedrock.
Buddleia, through two panes of
glass you are framed without flaw and the
collared doves that made nest
in your heights coo sweet melody in late summer's eve.

Buddleia, the wild flower planted at dark feet
is an offering. The wind charm hung off limb:
an offering too.
Midnight flower bloom in green parcel;
harbour grey bird wing, take wing under wing.
Coo sweet melody through rigid beak.
Buddleia, feel no need to return favours.

Buddleia, bodies lay under you in sunlight.
Filter midday through your leaves and
let the bodies press midnight flower bloomed
in green parcel flat against blue sky.
Collared doves land in unison,
remarked upon with a gesture. Buddleia,
you take this to mean love.

Buddleia, the panes of glass are too
hard for brittle skulls. Where grass becomes
paved lies three red spots, next to that,
a beak. Hands that planted offerings
now try to return your gift.
Midnight flower bloom in green parcel;
limbs mirror dark tracks on skin.

Buddleia, picture this:
It is raining, light rain but still rain.
There is someone knelt to your right, digging.

They finish digging and stand up,
walk across the garden, pick up
a stiff body of one of the collared doves.
You watch as they bury the body.
Watch as the rain adds to the wetness of tears.
Buddleia, midnight flower bloom in green parcel;
you will not hear sweet melody
                              this late summer eve.

Biff Pearson

Cuttings

'Poor Marion,' my mother-in-law shuffled into the garden room where I had been hiding with my coffee and magazine.

I took a slow, yogic breath of fortitude and disguised it as interest. 'Why? What's happened?' I didn't know Marion. I didn't care about Marion.

She lowered herself onto the wooden bench, I felt the thin slats bending under our combined weight. I shifted along subtly, and prepared for her speech. She sighed deeply through her nose. This wasn't regular sighing, this was big announcement sighing. This was sighing which said, what I'm about to say is very important so I'd better have your attention.
I waited.

'Well,' she began, once she chose to breathe normally again. 'Poor dear. It was her birthday yesterday and nobody remembered it. Nobody. Not even her daughter and, of course, she moved there to be near her.'

Why of course I wondered, but didn't say.
But, before I could stop myself.
'Did you remember?' I asked.

She shot a look at me over the top of her spectacles and something inside me, near my gut, shuddered with anticipation.

'Of course.' Her tone was careful, sidestepping my insinuation. She picked at a cleaver that clung to her trousers. The misinicule, hooked hairs ripped a hole the size of a lentil.

'That's why I called her.'
The thing in my gut lurched again and dared me to keep prodding.

'But you phoned her today. I thought you said her birthday was yesterday.'

I looked at her, but her profile gave little away. The thick lenses blurred her eyes from my view. I noticed that she was still bothering the hole in her trousers with a finger. It grew larger, to the size of a pomegranate seed, then a grape.

'Well, it was but I didn't call her yesterday.'
'Why not?' My innards contracted like a python around a

mouse.

She stood up, with alarming speed, and the bench squeaked in surprise. The hole in her trousers had become a ladder.

'I was wondering about the holly,' she said distantly, to the window. 'It really should come out. It's choking that rhododendron.'

I thought about how my sister, one Christmas time, had a go at some people in the park. They were snapping off red-berried branches to take home and decorate, I presumed.

'Stop that! Don't you know Holly trees only grow ten centimetres a year?'

I thought about mentioning it but my mother-in-law had already shuffled away.

Denise Monroe

Snakeskin

Pursed parchment held more marks than ruin did.
Bitter bruises nor shae slip away,
Shiny surface, searched for, but never found.
Teasing a taut grin of rotted makeup
Needled features held in steel rods might've helped.

She exists only in a rigid tense.
Held our frail innards in rash interest,
As only she is retained to a blank.
Sweet simpering smiles nailed in sharp angles,
For enigmas are always consistent.

Our sloppy smiles left us understandable.
As passionate furies we shriveled into the
Predictable, measurable, easily digestible-
Our pupils act too honest- we were the masses
Of soft mush even a fetus could swallow whole.

Her bricked-in pulse held no likeness to us.
Stoic, slow setting, unmalleable,
Without foul taunts and grunts of emotion.
Ridges for smiles and too watchful glass eyes
Yet I think I may worship her for that.

Jessica Lily Blissitt

Round Eyes

The eyes in between the leafy branches were round. They were large things, watching everything inquisitively with a kind of grace, pupils the midnight black that poured through you and engulfed everything around. The irises were the colour of oaken logs about to be thrown onto the fire. They looked like a permanent feature of the tree soon enough.

Leaves illuminated by the sun's rays from behind decorated the branches of the ash tree. This particular one was among the tallest in the forest, proud and old and sturdy. Its branches stretched into the image of any tree drawn onto a map to mark a forest, with the top curling, making a perfect curved edge. The trunk was peppered with pale scratches and chipped bark from smaller woodland animals that nibbled at its beauty. Each tree encircling it had the same mass of arms entangled with each other that they all may as well have been concealing a separate world for all I knew. I didn't bother penetrating the border to find out.

The forest floor was covered in small stones and seeds from the ashes and old leaves fallen on previous autumns. They formed a cushion that intruders, explorers and lost souls had to walk over. In pockets of light that penetrated the canopy, small plants were growing that could not reach past my knees. Most were a dark, hungry green and only had a couple of struggling leaves to express themselves with. I had to wade through them slowly, carefully treading, unable and unwilling to deliberately step on any one of them.

As another seed glided to the floor supported by the light wind, a bird whistled its tune from a branch far off in the distance. A musical trigger for a chorus of other birds to join, the sound echoing from one end of the forest to the other. I danced carefully through the crowd of trees towering over me to this song, slipping in between them like it was a game. My long cloak dragged over those flimsy plants as I walked, inviting an endless rustle. Eventually, I bundled the excess of material in my arms and elected to carry it, not wanting to spoil the music. My boots met the ground with a crunch every time regardless. Every so often I sniffed to clear my nose in the crisp air, the thick scent of sap enveloping my whole head afterwards. The auburn strands of my hair occasionally whipped my cheeks when the direction of my body and the wind stumbled into formation.

I arrived at a toppled tree lying across the foliage, having undoubtedly squashed it. The bark was rotted and home to what I could only imagine was a plethora of bugs. I clambered over it, its carcass heavy but shaking slightly beneath my feet. I plunged deeper into the forest's clutches, the trees gradually thickening. Less sunlight managed to reach the busy floor, obstructed by the intimacy of the trees in this part of the forest. As I walked under one branch, a sparrow darted off of it, soaring higher through a gap in the leaves and far from me. I stuttered to a stop before continuing with more consciousness to the volume of each step.

The crumbling remains of an old cottage sat among the trees a little way off. The stone bricks had tumbled down and were lying in front of the skeletal frame. The wooden beams that once made up the roof had collapsed inwards and smashed whatever was once left inside. A tree grew in the heart of the old building.

Behind the ruins, the compacted forest continued for a few hundred yards before opening up again like curtains in the early morning.

After traipsing along some more, the forest floor widened into a clearing. It was otherwise a bare clearing, with not many of the knee-high plants in the area, if any. There was, however, the unnatural addition of five bodies sprawled out over the circular area.

All of them were adults, as far as I could tell. Each of them were pale, the dark crimson flowing from them staining the leaves on the ground, draining them completely. A swarm of flies buzzed a frenzy above each of them, especially the man at the back. He was lying on his back, opposite to the others, and his stomach was torn down the middle. Out of the gash spilled some bright red entrails, some over his stomach, some managed to make it to the floor, some were a few feet away. It was as if a pit of snakes were nesting over his dead body.

The man closest to my feet had a beard, greasy and matted. He had deep grooves cut all over his body, his clothes torn to shreds and stained so red that the brown of his cloak was more like patches on the spread of blood. The woman next to him had her head slashed straight off. Her tangle of raven locks had rolled a good distance away from the rest of her body. Blood leaked at tidal levels from her neck stump, creating a shallow pool just below. The final two bodies were somehow more sliced up than hers, however. Both of them had limbs scattered all over the clearing that I could not be able to distinguish which part belonged to which body. At the centre of the circle, a single, severed hand was lying palm-up, still fixed in a firm claw, once tensed in rage, now stuck that way with rigor.

Across the clearing, in the trees opposite, was a familiar pair of round, brown eyes. I smiled.

Kiera Stibbons

The Waterfall

We only became ourselves just yesterday; the people in the photographs are strangers. It doesn't matter if we take them down.

A hand is not an eraser it is just a hand;
it is not capable of erasing. A man is not Jesus he is just a man;
he is not capable of miracles. But that is precisely the problem.
A problem is not a message like a gift disguised. It is just a problem,
it is not capable of pre-planning. A lie is not a necessity,
or a means justified, it is just a lie,
it is not capable of redemption.

It's a supernova sunrise, and we're sitting on a hilltop and waiting for God
to make the day explode, hoping to catch a piece of the good life,
when it all starts caving in. But the supernova is not the song Heaven sings when she wakes up from her sleep,
it is just an explosion. The only thing it is capable of is exploding;
It is an action hero designed without the saviour part. It explodes and you have to pick up the pieces.

Is it dead? You ask the silence.
If it's dead then it will die. It is both already dead
and not dead yet. It is both dead and alive. Dying is a complicated process,
it's not always so cut and dry. Thank god for poison.
Poison is a guarantee, a home remedy, it is not capable of asking too many questions.
Can it be saved? You ask again.
If it's saved then it will die. You can only save it
if it's not in need of saving. It is both saved
and in need of saving. It is both safe and at risk. It is both already dead

and not dead yet. Dying is a complicated process.
Regardless, we can't all be saviours. Thank god for poison.
Thank god for destroyers, it's not the saviours I like. I like the eyes that shine
like blue lights jumping highway signs. The only option is full throttle.
The only option
is a total loss of control.

You are not a destroyer, you are just hungry,
you are both already dead and not dead yet. I'm not a saviour,
there's no such thing. It is both already dead and not dead yet.
We're in the waterfall, and there's nowhere to go but down;
we are both already drowned and still drowning. We are both already dead
and not dead yet. It's no fun learning to swim
when drowning's the only option. We are both drowned and resuscitated.
Dying is a complicated process.

Lucy Cundill

Seasons Change

Autumn: leaves change colour and fall. Dying and rotting away. Trees are preparing for a new production cycle, while the grass becomes cluttered with a scattered rustling assortment of shapes and sizes. The weather becomes bitter: gone are the warm days of British summer weather. Hello to the sun beaming down on a thick white blanket, not powerful enough to melt it. Plants – once standing as tall and proud as a soldier – bow their heads as they perish. A cycle of life, in the eyes of Mother Nature's beauty.

The only thing that doesn't change is when you want the sun to shine, it rains and rains and rains.

Max Wrigley

Love and a Can of Worms

The brutal mist of loneliness
Flooded through the mountain lake.
The salmon, haddock and the hake
Swam so acrimonious.
And something rotted in my core
That I had never known before.
The air was crisp and clear, awake,
But I felt disharmonious.

I opened up a can of worms
And threw away my holy book,
Impaled my passion on a hook -
I planned to kill it as it squirmed.
And with love on the fishing line,
And static playing in my mind,
I stilled the compass with a look.
Nothing else could be infirm.

The fish were jumping well that day,
Five thousand, and a mermaid's purse.
I stored my catch inside a hearse
And searched for something strong to say.
Then, having cried "I am! I am!",
I sealed my feelings in a can,
And gave it to the universe.
I let my love be cast away.

I carried with me, that day forth,
A knapsack full of broken souls.
Love still lingers at the poles,
But I never venture so far north.
My can of worms is sealed still.
(The key is in a sleeping pill).

And now my hut is dark and cold.
And, too, my life has lost its course.

Samuel Glynn

Advert for the Latest Apocalypse

It had been ash, and would be sickly; a
zeppelin downed in London, steel-tumour clad and dragged
from the beds of an allotment - churning dirt, and slowly. So was
the New World Born.
    'Look at these babies! 1/2/3
and the conveyer-belt's away – spittin' them fast
and blasting out a future that's never been known;
new shoes! – cellophane creatures – new car!
- vibrating like a phallus -
Napalm! And a high-tech, newly formed
spryer-than-the-last-one preacher who's got teeth to offer
this time round; pearly gates of his speech tattoo
the American promise to the ground, and the only shadow
to falls from a (spick n' span) hairline, SO coiffured
to neatly tour suburbia's lawns -
    and over the pond? Why, Albion Ultima! Gloria in
Excelsis Lizzie; cus' aren't miniskirts the key to rolling high
Regina
of the streets? Be hip like a stone! Or have hips like a stone, cus'
Jagger's
a catch, jagged as a pinprick in the cultural map! So, pick up a
paper
- it's waiting and aching for you to get your crayons, caper in
colour   across the front page:
'Keep Calm and Carry on
Buying. If the end is caustic or
I'm gonna sear, I wanna be
smokin' hot when it gets here."

Seb Gale

What Can You Say?

what can you say
Is all I can think to say
when my cousin's other uncle's girlfriend
is crying into my arms
at my brother's wedding
because her cat has died
and she can't be at home to hold it

she is sobbing violently
and all attempts to hand her a tissue have failed
her mascara slowly dripping onto my shirt
my parents are outside, taking photos with the couple
and hopefully wondering where I've got to

Silas Hand

On the Line

Chapter 2

The Fool

Sad clown seeking clown
No homo, just bro shit like
Kissing and crying

I love you fish boy
You are a ceramic fish
And I'm a woman

Your silly throne creaks
While I dance a painted fool
Inky fingers still

Reverse Medusa
Snakes writhing inside my brain
Are they good or bad?

Clem Hailes

Creative Writing Society

Love Letter

And if I had the time, or the rope or the timbers you would ask why I had strung up a wishbone necklace to give to you, you, why the kitchenlit night amid the low scented darkness. Why I hoped the mute wishbones in a greasying string. And, thinking, somewhere- why the birds did suddenly appear, and why anything else, strewn all around us, stooped up, presented found into my tremoring palms to give, directed into my palms for your palms. And for looking into your eyes. Why any green shard, or beach stone, why and lump or shape, any object, looking, dawning, waking, and stretching, its head contorted in dawning, stretching or yawning, why any groped-through thing that in my looks links and looks, and echoes with you. Why any new or old, why any of these de-submerged objects wouldn't do.
And I hope I would say: those things, those cut-through things I know, I give you them dreaming I think as we would walk in the winds, the field, the broad, the blue sky and clouds looking, then looking away. Like they are leaving us to ourselves even as they shine and are in the wind and windy sun and daylight. New-rocked things, turned over as birds in wind all turned and rocked over, while the broad we walked on rolled over in rushes. These pieces, they could be gripped, they could be gathered, gazed-at, laughed-at, and inspected, you inspecting them and I would inspect you, in them, in them as they look like they reflect, reflect you, in your palm. In their colours, in their shadows and their lights, and their cracks and smoothness and in their feel you would be in them.
But they would amalgamate, in the cross, in the air that breathes this jump, one way, one look and after another, the flutter of the chicken's wing in goldsun, to a plate. they would fill up and bustle and rattle in your bag. Since they would amalgamate and spread, lose themselves, in misplacement, or in your tide draining out of the wet sand ponds, or in your breath, or in sighs. I make you though I have no gold links, I have made you a wishbone necklace.

I did not snap the wishbone twig, I could eat no meat nor scrape carcasses, and so I found these birds' bones, unhaunted, no longer haunted now and I give you these bones and their wishes; these wishes unsnapped now, to you. It is very light around you when you put it on. No windy wishes in the wind, the wishbones curved like tuning forks, no windy wishes caught and spent in wind like stunned birds in reducing flight at ash of day. These wishes, though still undone, these wishes, which are all my wishes, though you can wish with them what you must. These wishes, I give them in these found and given bones, all of them these un-broken wishes are with you now.

Alex Eaglestone

Astrid and Askeladden

Inspired by Edvard Munch's 'The Sick Child'

"Don't be sad, mama."

Astrid's mother will not meet her eye. The girl's red hair is plastered to her milky forehead. A sweet, cloying smell hangs in the air. Astrid wants to ask her mother to open the window, just a crack, just for a minute, but knows she'd refuse. Bad for a fever. The room is warmed by a fire, flickering in the hearth. It hisses the odd orange ember. It's too warm: her mother is wasting fuel again.

Outside, snowflakes land on the windowpanes and immediately turn to water, dribbling their way downwards and making tracks through the condensation. When she is alone, Astrid likes to watch them, placing bets on which one will reach the bottom first. She doesn't like it when they conjoin, it confuses her.

She turns her head to the left, to the mirror on the wall beside the window. She can see herself over her mother's shoulder. Her reflection is her constant company. Beneath the sallow sheen of her skin, her eyes burn with the intensity of the damned. Her free hand travels to the silver crucifix around her neck. The metal feels hot to the touch. She swallows. Her throat is parched.

"Mama," she whispers.

Her mother looks up. Her eyes are sadness ringed with blue. Downturned mouth, fine lines. Worry on her brow. Brown bun, streaked with grey. She's still clutching Astrid's left hand.

"Some water, *takk*," She croaks.

Her mother nods, stands up to her full height, crosses the room in two long steps. Pours water from the jug on the dresser, and returns. The room is dim, lit only by the small fire and a paraffin lamp. Her mother is wearing a dark dress. Her pale skin gives the appearance of a disembodied head and hands.

Astrid takes a sip from the glass which has been held out to her. She shifts her weight on the pillow supporting her back. Her joints ache. She wants to go out and walk, but Winter has gathered its short days and bitter cold. Her lungs couldn't take it.

An icy wind rattles the glass. Now, despite the heat, the heavy snow is beginning to collect in the corners of the window like dust. Her mother follows her gaze.

"Maybe it will be better by tomorrow," her mother says, but they both know it's not true.

"Yes, maybe."

"You could even visit the Anderssons in a few weeks, if we get a nice day."

"Yes." She tries to smile.

"It's almost spring really, when you think about it. And then, once it's spring, it's not even that much longer until we can go cloudberry picking again. You'll come with me, won't you?" her words are falling out faster and faster now "Magnus gets bored, and Ingrid can't carry the basket yet, or she might trip, and we can't have tha-"

"Yes, mama. I will."

Her mother smiles and smoothes the hair from her forehead.

A silence settles. Astrid can hear her family's feet creaking on the wooden floorboards in the rest of the house. She counts them: two heavy treads and one lighter tread. She knows who it is when they pass by. Her big brother's loping stride. Her little sister's uneven trot. Her father's heavy thud. At least they seem to have made peace with her passing. She only sees her mother now, and only in the evenings. Only when the last of the sun's weak light has long since faded over the horizon, travelling west. Only when her mother's bones ache and her hands are red and cracked. Astrid is a ghost in this house. She haunts them.

Her mother's hands clutch at Astrid's, rough skin brushing against clammy softness. She rubs Astrid's hands as if she could rub the life back into them.

"Shall I tell you about Askeladden and the forest troll?"

Astrid's heard the tale a hundred times. But her mother always embellishes it differently. Sometimes Askeladden's brothers go back with him into the forest. Sometimes Askeladden's cheese is too ripe to fool the troll into thinking it's a rock. And sometimes Askeladden is sent by the troll to chop wood and threatens to bring the whole forest instead.

"I'm too old," she says, but she knows her mother will tell it anyway, and secretly she wants her to.

Her mother takes a deep breath and begins: "*Det var en gang...*"

Anna Rumsby

How to Love I

brush tart all over,
simmer gently,
ladle by ladle,
until very smooth,
just turning golden.

now the exciting part:
gently knead,
make a quick pickle,
gently squeeze;
no need to go crazy, though.

keep an eye on it,
as needed to avoid sticking
(you don't want total mush).

[she's] Softened, slumped,
needs special treatment,
too dark for your liking.
don't unfold yet or [she] will crack -

when the time's up,
pull gently away;
cut in half from top to bottom -
tear off and discard.

How to Love II

make shallow, lengthwise cuts,
then use your fingers
[to] crush [him] into pea-size pieces -
be as gentle and slow as you like,
this will bring it up to speed.

he will be soft to the touch,
still wet and a little sticky.
beat on high-speed,
until flavours have melded;
then add [his] zest.

[he] will look thick and creamy
begin to crystallise and Harden
(just make sure you smash each piece).

reduce heat to medium-low and
simmer gently;
keep an eye on it,
until fragrant, then squeeze in.

go under and over in a figure of eight,
stop just before you feel you should;
shake off any excess -
serve and enjoy!

Clara Ehlers

East London, June, 2016

I used to get unexplainable green smears on my school shirt, laid down in the park, on the soft mounds of cut grass going rotten in the cool shade of the chestnut tree with the football stuck in it. I was in the arms of a boy I liked then but hate now, I should have been revising exam material, books about men and mice and meaningless life, chemical equations and algebraic formulas but I wasn't interested, everyone remembers it as the best summer of their childhood but the country just voted to leave? And bodies were washing up on tourist beaches like driftwood or rubbish, being found by Pokemon Go playing kids, I couldn't waste a moment of my extended summer, laid in the park during school hours, skipping meals to get drunk faster, soon I'd be far away on the other side of the European border, sat in a concrete house with no T.V. or Wifi, no news is good news they say don't they? Burning my bottom on the marble-ledged balcony, the sweat on my fingers stuck to the book pages as I looked up at the refugee boys stranded on my grandmother's roof, shovelling cement to feed their sisters and painting the walls a shade of honey, one of them had ice blue eyes and a warm yellow smile, he told me in his quiet words about his favourite books and half done degree in medicine and interrupted dreams and then I wandered around the village in the midday pressure cooker heat looking for the cold water spring I could have sworn was somewhere close by, local women stopped on the sandy track and asked me whose wife I was and where had I come from? Why did my hair shine around my shoulders? And I didn't really answer, at some point I visited a dying man's house, the same women were there, brewing little glass cups of black tea and tiptoeing between the men lounging on the mismatched patchwork carpet like the stray cats in the stinking government bins outside, my aunties led me to the women and opened the Qur'an on page four hundred and something and my mind wandered over and picked up the story of the three little school boys all named after prayers, their teacher demanded they recite their name sake and cheeky Yasin who is six goddamn pages long quipped that his nickname was

Subhaneke, which is barely a mouthful of words, in the corner of the room one of the children's computers was glowing blue in the background, a Facebook feed on display, I watched a video of a cluster bomb exiting an aircraft ten thousand feet above, decimate a village, not too far from there, on houses not too different. It played on a loop over and over and over.

Elif Soyler

My Sky is Not Blue

It used to be cream with a skirting board
pinched at the edge
and strands of sticky tape forgotten
from old Christmas decorations.

The tinsel would hang in smiles
around the edge until I decided
I wanted to cling to those grins
but the tape ripped off the paint
and tinsel wilted beside my broken arm.

'Almond Cream No. 620'
A matt cream base with warm undertones
was bleached by the energy efficient bulbs
my mum would buy
that washed the living room
into an overexposed photo.
It made my friends wince
and I started complaining of headaches.

We had a problem with damp
that ate into the corners
I used to think it was a spider's nest
until it morphed into a menacing face
mottled with black eyes and teeth
that fed on cream paint and white light.
My dad would buy
'Dettol Mould and Mildew Remover'
and the mouldy monster faded into coffee stains.

Now I look up at my sky
the bits of sticky tape have rotated
as I am not allowed to stand on chairs,
and the bulbs have been replaced with
'Warm White Energy Savers.'

The damp worsens each year
as the stains become espresso
and the chemicals my Dad uses
are always the same.
My sky is not blue
it is cream with chipped
paint and black spots,
the sticky tape is laughing at me
and the stained corners are closing in.
Now before me is an empty room

and my sky is no longer mine.

Emma Bullen

Mini Smarties

Nanny and Gan-Gan gave us
Mini smarties
As children

We had smarties in between
Ice cream in the garden
All four cousins
Sat on the bench
A little longer

In the arms of grandparents
A little longer
Stayed in the sun
A little longer
Was all we asked for
Before going to sleep
[lie down on the bed]

Sometimes I can still smell
The warm bedclothes
In mum's old bedroom
I can still smell
The watercolour paints
Gan-Gan gave us all
[Gan-Gan was an artist]

Keep pulling me back
To warm photographs
And strong, safe arms
Golden days, caramel afternoons
Through all the birthdays
All the times sat in a bucket
In dead mid-year heat

How happy we are

As grandchildren
And grandparents
And I wonder
[though I know]
Whether he is proud
Wherever grandparents go
To watch over us
How happy we were.

I thought of all this
In the jumper I bought in Dublin
[navy wool and cosy neck]
Coloured bumps through it
Like the mini smarties I had
As a child.

Erin Ketteridge

Mum's Favourite Game

"You can tell a lot about a person by the shoes on their feet"
It was a game we'd often play.
Perfect for coffee shop musings and restaurant giggles over pinot whilst scanning for first dates and last dates and 'we're just friends' dates.
And, as I recently found out,
Late night commutes on rattly trains.

So that's where I find myself;
The 7:32 from Paddington to Poplar,
Complete with bleary tear stained windows,
Flickering fluorescents,
And the rowdy print of balding tube seats.

The shoppers of Oxford Street shuffle in.
Lipstick and hair and this season's latest gear,
White McQueen's still pristine, of course.
Insta likes, trips to Bali with Daddy's money and brunch with the besties.
Eh, perhaps that's a little shallow of me.
Watch. I'll do better on the next one.

The hipsters of Shoreditch stroll on not long after,
Scuffed doc martens tap to a band you will never have heard of.
They probably run some start up that rids the ocean of rubbish,
Bet their beards are better tended to than our oceans ever will be,
Maybe also lose that topknot,
You look more like a shih tzu than a model for GQ, darling.
Wow. I have had a bad day.

I look around the train,
Be nice.
Polished brogues. Great.
City man, 2.5 kids and a white picket fence,
Wife probably runs the annual PTA bake sale. Wait.

Odd socks.
He's shagging his secretary.
My disapproving eyebrows bore into him.

We've stopped.
A glance out the window throws me off completely.

A man with no shoes.
Raw pink slabs, frozen to the pavement.

My inner spiel of judgement comes to a grinding halt.
His feet stare back at me, and still nothing.
A whole novel, but with no ink on the pages for it to be read.
No detail or embellishments to draw the reader in.

It dawns on me.

This train is a means to an end.
A means to be dry, a means to be fed,
And my ticket permits me to be a player of this game, not played.

There's no-one telling them to mind the gap.
Who will care if they fall through the cracks?

Those feet can't even stand on a street corner,
Let alone behind a yellow line.
I think I've found a problem with your game mum.
No more giggling over white wine.

Jess Miller

Not Me

A moony, realist tone heaping in your throat
and you gulping down. Your plans happened to be
rotten splinters. The obstinate look in your eyes
is gone, but I can still catch
a furtive glimpse of clairvoyance
stirring your insides
when I let you hold my palms.
You don't try to involve me, slowly force me,
in your life anymore. You don't square
your smile between sly dimples
or tug blighted words behind my ear.
There's no more ear left for you
to bite, and chew, and spit out.
The attempt to convert me
into a post-impressionist
has now become stale.
No rosemary and no roses.
You dare not foist any on me, you dare not
call for anything in return.
A bath of luna and siesta
to spoil my wounds, or reading
"Blood Wedding" out loud
was not enough.
I did not want to be your blade of grass.

But now you listen,
and in the unruly cacophony of the kitchen
the radio yields, (a last opportunity):

When the cat gut binds my ankles to your bedstead /
That ain't love, no that ain't love.

Oihane García

Oystercatcher

Like this, the same words over and over
as I hanged myself with his black tie. No,
he untied it for me then twisted it taut
and pushed the knot up, Like this.

We looked just alike; in the mirror
I saw the parts of him that made me,
shoulders small but ready to fill my father's
suit. I longed to wear one with him,

one like his from his first interview,
first date, wedding, honeymoon,
moments reflective of his. Dad stood jubilant
on his happiest days, now framed on the mantle.

I practised in his suit on cold days, stamping in his boots,
buttons up and cuffs rolled: it smelled of paperwork.
I would walk up the drive, smile his ten tooth smile:
I thought I could interview the world.

I had only one day in my father's suit;
too young to afford one I stood in his,
still ten sizes too big, our family's hands
slowly browning him with soil.

Oliver Shrouder

Electric Razor

Afterwards
    you would hang slovenly off
the bathroom hook,
teeth filled with
        stolen hairs
never washed out.

You were his.
    the water does not run
    the hairs do not grow
        or fall;
only he could move you.

You no longer sing
        cicada-happy to wake me.
He would
    brush your blades,
    flush the dark away
and return newly:
    I would hold his face like wet clay.
He gleamed like our cutlery.

        You gloom
like a red moon.

You hang falling
        but for your cord
like a millstone mid-plunge

    searching
for a new face to tend

Oliver Shrouder

Storytime

"Do you want to hear a story?"
were the most exciting
six words
my father ever uttered,
as he sat
in his comfortable,
cushioned chair,
a delicate cup of earl grey
brushing his lips,
being careful not to burn
his tongue with the hot water.

I sat in his lap
patiently awaiting transportation,
within seconds
I was no longer on earth,
I was flying past
galaxies and constellations,
wiggling around the stars,
and laughing with pure joy.

I was gullible,
in a good way.
In the most perfect way,
my innocence my shield,
my imagination a secret weapon,
unlocking doors and opening up new horizons.

In hindsight,
I realise now
he never was an originalist,
but that didn't matter,
it never mattered to me.
His power to spark new ideas
for stories I'd later recreate

fascinated me,
my everlasting interest
came from his ability
to tell a story
with such enthusiasm,
my favourite characters
embarking on new quests
and challenges.
With every word came a new level of excitement,
my eyes widening,
and mouth dropping to the floor.

Struggling to sleep,
I toss and turn,
giddy with anticipation
until the morning,
asking: "what'll happen next?"
A moment that,
in my head,
will always last forever.

Ray Khawaja

Evelyn: Extract from a Novel

Nick

My mother won't confirm it, but I have a distinct memory of building Marble Arch. Shaping a small model out of sugar on a café table, adding a sculpture on the top, deciding against it. Slaving in my university room to finish it, sweating awake and in my sleep, changing my sheets every morning, going back to work with a hammer, teeth ripper, cloth, chisel. I let you do one gleeful revolution through its three arches when it was finished, twisting a figure of eight, doing it in a run, kissing me after, before I shrunk it down small enough that you were able to open a cavity and tuck it in my chest like a locket. You would still run rings through it when I least expected.

I had been keeping you barred for a time for my personal safety by the day I came home and found you setting your life on fire. There are things that are called crimes of passion; things that are done with the world stained red, in heat, against all reasonable will, crimes which can be repented for. You were not capable.

Among the flames in the garden that hissed and bit when I tried to come close enough to salvage anything – fuck off, prick, there's a resurrection happening here – were your birth certificate, debit card, the gas and electric bill, a pair of hairdressing scissors, your best paintings and your mobile phone. I bought you a new one the next week when your agent eventually called me to ask why he couldn't get through to you.

I think, if I hadn't come home early, if I hadn't held you round the waist in a way that made you scream at me and try to scratch lost into my cheek, in a way that you thought was prevention but was really self-preservation, you would've thrown yourself in. To burn, melt, expire, repent, to stumble new-born and phoenix-like three days later from the spent ash.

When Gavin and Sam are asleep, I open that small door in my chest, take out the arch, and try to fit your Star of David through an archway like a skeleton key in a lock. I say your name like it's a resurrection. I say your name like there are parts of my body which don't belong to you. As if, with every invocation, it becomes statistically more likely that something of you might defy law and rise from ash.

There is still a pocket space unhealed, starting in my lower back, a tunnel of unstitched tissue up to my neck for your arm, your hand, to wrap around the familiar pull-cord of my tongue, and use your mouth to make me speak.

***

Ink

It's somehow late February before he notices that there are hyacinths growing out of the bathroom sink. He's spent so long staring at her ghost face that when he looks in the bathroom mirror he's shaving her cheeks, so I suppose he can be forgiven for being short-sighted.

Hyacinths start to come up between the bathroom floor tiles, from under the socket in the hallway chandelier, out of the utility room tap and the third shelf from the floor in his bookshelves. He tells Gavin and Sam to make sure they shake their shoes outside the front door to escape carrying them elsewhere and dealing with an infestation – he sets up a tank to collect rainwater and takes pruning scissors into the downstairs cloakroom to stop them taking root in his pockets.

Hyacinths begin growing in the window. At first, I think they've woven their way up the wall outside despite this being December and this house being a crypt, but they're coming out of the waterproof coating on the inside, mostly purple and sometimes blue.

Insipid little things in half-bloom like they got partway there, like a semi that no one wanted to fuck. They come up between Reuben's hairs in the rug and he douses them with weedkiller which does nothing but makes Sam cough and the house smell like chlorine.

Gavin worries that they'll have to dig up the foundations of the house – 'bamboo roots can spread ages away from the plant, what if they're like bamboo?' He asks while he and Sam rip them out of the landing carpet but never get to veins.

'They're not like bamboo,' Nick tells him, but the crown moulding in his bedroom has cracked to let flowers in. Gavin doesn't need to see that. His poor divorcee heart couldn't take the sight of all that affection. At night the wind rattles the doors in their frames like it's telling-not-asking them to open up and hand over their prisoners.

Contrary to popular belief, they're not the kind of flowers to share thrones. Nick's mattress begins to smell sweet and when he cuts a gash in the side, hyacinths have wound their way around the springs.

Shannon Clinton-Copeland

Creative Writing Society

Chapter 3

The Bard

Vines choke my tower
A bed barely built for one
Could safely hold two

If I ruled the sea
We'd bob softly through the blue
Brainless and carefree

Your reckless tide
Rushes over my little shore
Jewels littered with nails

What is it, my head?
So many thoughts swimming there
A soup of intrigue

Clem Hailes

Creative Writing Society

Smoke

Thumping steps, louder and louder until the bed is jolting under me. I scramble to pull a shirt on, I don't want Harry to see the puckered scar over my heart.
"Morning, shithead!" Harry bellows as he explodes through the door, "Rise and shiiiine!"
"It's four in the fuckin' afternoon, Haz. I've been up for hours." I try and scowl at him but can't stop a smirk as he brandishes a joint at me like we're about to fence.
"You. Me. Smoke. Now."
"I've quit, Harry. I'm gonna get a job." I'm still talking as Harry hoots with derisive laughter.
"Sure, sure, sure. I'll see you in the garden in ten."
He departs as melodramatically as he arrived, leaving a familiar scent marijuana and body odour in his wake. I blow a sharp breath through my nose. Fuck him for doubting me. This time I'm quitting for real.
My attic room is stuffy in the summer heat. I pull my top back off and lob it out of sight, letting my fingers wander to the old wound on my chest. The outline of the pacemaker pushes up my skin like an alien egg about to hatch. Dust swirls in jagged sunbeams.

I'm eighteen again, sweating under blazing August sunshine. My whites are pristine but beneath them my heart is hammering against my ribs, an untamed animal attacking the bars of its cage. I'm aware of eyes, so many eyes, all zeroed in on me as I take my place at the stumps. I don't want to be here. I told Dad I wasn't ready. The bowler begins his wind up and the sweat from my palms threatens to soak through my gloves. I hear Dad booming my name over the crowd, strident and inevitable. The ball fires at me, impossibly fast. An explosion in my chest. Darkness.
I wake up in a hospital bed, concerned faces swimming around me. My body feels tight, strange. Mum is weeping, smiling through her tears at me. Dad has red eyes but just frowns.

I pull my fingers away from the scar. I'm staring at the cricket bat, half-hidden behind a mound of dirty clothes. Livid blotches stain its face, the scars of many hard-fought battles.

The memory still rattles around my head, vivid and cruel. I grab Vivaldi's Four Seasons from the shelf and set it on the record player, moving the needle to where I know "Winter" begins.

Dad and I used to listen to this record. He preferred "Summer", hopelessly optimistic as it is.

Winter's opening strains leak out of the battered old speaker, bittersweet and lonely. I breathe out my tension in a whoosh and fall back onto my bed. I sink into the violins' lament.

Raucous quarrelling from the garden shatters my reverie.

"Jimmyyy," Harry's voice floats up, "Come out and play."

"Jimmy's not in right now, can I take a message?" I drawl, trying to keep my tone light and easy. I hear laughter.

I'm not the same as the rest of the boys. They don't have a safety net. They really are from the wrong side of the tracks. They're good about it though, pretending not to notice when my forced slang clangs through the conversation like a dropped anvil.

I chose to run away – away from the stifling embrace of studying Law and county cricket and the whole fucking life Dad planned for me. I don't regret that. Do I? Problem is, I'm not running towards anything. Now what? Living on the dole in this rotting old squat isn't a long-term solution. A void where a life should be, occupies my chest, a black hole that feels like it will suck me in unless I fill it with weed and pills and booze and…

I dig my nails into my thighs. I force myself to listen to the music.

Smoke and chatter curl in through the window, morphing together into a beckoning finger. Harry and Lee are down there with some of their old uni mates. All I have to do is descend and I can dampen the clamour in my head for a few hours.

No. Not this time.

The whiff of smoke triggers a long-suppressed memory.

The bonfire looked a hundred feet tall in front of our bone-white picket fence, a blazing column that was converting a whole life into smoke. I built it with school-books, cricket whites and job applications. With expectations, judgements and crushing pressure.
"James! What the fuck is this?!"
It was the angriest I'd ever seen Dad, which is saying something. He lurched around the inferno towards me, pulled his mobile phone out then turned to me again. His eyes were wild.
"I can't do it any more Dad..." I don't know if he could even hear my murmur over the roar and crackle. "I'm sorry. I can't."
He finally inspected my face and his fury seemed to evaporate. "James...?" He looked utterly bewildered and for the first time ever I felt sorry for him. Then I burnt that too and walked down the drive for the last time.

I heave myself out of bed and pick up the old bat. My fingertips find craters too small for the eye to pick out. I'd nearly added it to the bonfire but couldn't quite bring myself to. Dad gave it to me when I finally made first team, what should have been the proudest moment of my life. And I had been proud...but only because he wanted me to be.
He never stopped pushing me. Not even after I died in the cruel August sunshine.
A life of smoke. Purposeless, amorphous....cancerous.
The closing notes of "Winter" fade away and the record player resets itself with a comforting click. My cheeks are wet. I drop the bat and shamble over to flip the record. Harry wrestles with someone I don't know out on the scrubby lawn, breathless laughter bursting from the tussle. I can't help but smile. I'll go down for a moment, just to be polite. I won't even smoke.

***

Harry crashes through my door but I interrupt him.
"Not interested Haz, I'm really quitting this time."

He rolls his eyes and leaves, laughing. Familiar heat rises in my chest, a familiar itch growing in my skull. This time. This time...

Alec Goldstone

Foreign Land - A Journal Entry

And breathe... What am I so afraid of? So afraid I cannot stay in a crowded room for one minute before fleeing. To safety. To my comfort zone.

    I try to push those fears away as I tread up the stairs, slowly, deliberately. A faint noise resonates in the distance. "Hello!" I freeze. My attention instantly shifts, fixates on bringing my emotions under control. My wide eyes shift from the carpeted floor to a woman standing proudly with a clipboard. Coming here was a bad idea. I fashion a polite smile and sign in.

    The noise, once a muffled murmur, has transformed, mutated, accelerated to great proportions. My mouth suddenly dry, I regurgitate saliva which briefly moistens my mouth. My breathing increases, heart races, stomach trembles. A hauntingly familiar sensation. "Let's get this over with", I sympathetically utter to myself, already defeated before the battle has begun.

    I look up and read `Vandenberg Hall`. My sorry eyes slowly drop to take in the source of the thunderous noise: wall to wall people and pumping music. Its vibrations course through my body. I readjust my top, the skin of my body rising in temperature as blood pummels to the surface, veins now visible, protruding, leaving an embossed appearance.

I cross the border, one foot followed cautiously by the other. I know I don't belong. My gaze shifts from one location to the next, never settled. An abundance of information to take in, to process. As I make my way from table to table, I can feel the eyes of others, judging, contemplating if I'm a fit for their club. "No" is the visible response, despite the tight smiles I receive. Past experience tells me so.

    I feel like I'm being auctioned off, my humiliation doubled by the lack of bidders. I hurriedly yet smoothly manoeuvre my way through the dancing motion of the full crowd. All my senses temporarily focus on the forever exit, blocking out the periphery. I stumble past another male. He too looks just as out of place, for we have unknowingly landed on foreign land. I escape, not looking back at the now prisoner of the damned.

David Davies

Freddie Starr Ate My Hampster

A love letter to coming of age as the world ends around you.

You know, in those days
There was no such thing as a twenty-four hour news cycle.
We lived in shades of grey,
Smothered between black and white
Newspaper sheets and if you read behind
The lines you realised that even though you could vote
Now, it didn't make much fucking difference.

On trips into town you had half-empty buckets
Shook in your face, sunken eyes in doleful pits
That had bugger all else
And well, neither did you. A lady
Pissed her trousers on the high street as the big
Red button burned a hole in the sky, spitting
Image of rat people, scurried under sirens.

You know, in these days, we get
Sixteen notifications a day on average.
You've reached the saturation point.
Terrified at thirteen, numbed by twenty,
Dad lost his job to a machine,
The year before I went to uni.
The lady's not for turning, U-turning, turning, U-turning on

Butterless ham sandwiches for state scrounging kids,
Assembled in some technicolour kitchen come factory.
Chased the Muslim mum down the street to swap
For endangered tuna mayonnaise and the guy
In a chair rammed a cashpoint customer.
Hungry men brushed their teeth with bottled water
In the queue at Dover on Christmas Eve.

You know, in these days
It's entertainment.
We don't watch the news at dinnertime anymore.

Elif Soyler

Stutter

Your call sounds like red slits -
Kissing my throat and it
Claws to rip a nipple
Pierced with one of your index fingers
Why did it surprise me
Your devotion to wet, peeling skin.

Let's pretend to aid this foolish fancy
When I smile it aches and wilts from spouting happiness
Laughing is a mellifluous chuckle, not shrill plastic stuck to our backs.
Strutting should be for giddy breathlessness at my age
Can stripping be an option? Might as well add whore to the list.

I am stripped, bleached, torn, puckered up
To sizzle on the spit of a glossy magazine.
Needle arch my back and rip across my nose to cleanse me.
Lust, sweat and satin curl around our embrace
To gnaw on my organs, caress my burning skin.
I am not in control, but I see the appeal.

But I do not fear this. A worse day is coming.
When
My lips twitch to pout, shreds of vermillion flake off
Eyes, sewn over to sparkle in long seductive lashes on my
Backless tops that reveal freshly picked skin too soft for daylight
Hair pulled and teased until it falls in stringy noodles,
Will be the day my soul is rammed into a bodega bin.

Jessica Lily Blissitt

Three Letters in the Pandemic

48 Caterham Street
10th Circle of Hell
YN6 9TP
1st November 2020

███

26 Dawlish Road
The Abyss
NP4 7YX

Dear Comrade,
Today someone asked me whether I thought I was more relaxed this year or last. I had to think.
This year there's been so much violence and stupidity and death in the news. There's a global pandemic, a failing economy, broken politicians, and no hope of changing any of the above. It's the closest we've ever been to an apocalypse on Earth and neither Christ, King Arthur or Owain Glyndŵr have shown up yet. All of this is reason enough to label this year the most stressful yet.
But then I remembered last year: our first year at university. I thought of freshers' and its 'false glitter'.
My flatmates agreed. We are so much more relaxed this year than the last. Isn't that strange?
You know Allen Ginsberg's poem, Footnote to Howl, where he describes bums and madmen and asylums and railroads and hipsters and suffering as holy?
Well, I was thinking about it and that's what the first year of university is like.
In all its madness, desperation, discovery, sweat, grime, confusion and chaos – there is something quite miraculous about it. In all its sordidness, exhaustion and mania – it's miraculous – every second of it: a blaring, panic-stricken, unbelievable miracle.
How aware do you find you are of COVID these days? It's

strange. I think I'm less in tune than I was in the first wave. Everything is so disruptive – and yet – as I sit here with a bottle of wine and four-pack of spaghetti hoops clutched under either arm, I am painfully aware that not even a pandemic, in all its restrictions, can put a halt to student life.

Well, on that note, I will reaffirm my statement that the only things that matter in this world are: red wine, good friends and poetry. It is enough, for now, to be content with this.

Stay well,

Creative Writing Society

26 Dawlish Road
The Abyss
NP4 7YX

18th December 2020

████████
48 Caterham Street
10th Circle of Hell
YN6 9TP

Comrade,
What a fucking year.
My social life has progressed to drinking in public places and peeing in nearby forests. The other night I accidentally left two wine glasses out on a blue plastic bin outside my house. I found them the next morning, bleary-eyed and hungover. It looked like a fucking modernist masterpiece.
Social "triumphs" aside, I've been swimming in essay central. There is little process. You scream until you make a song.
'You can't just write about death in every essay.' Someone said.
'I can,' I replied, draining my glass, 'and I will.'
As you know, I like to vacillate between hard-core Catholicism and full-blown nihilism. Recently, my faith had been waning and I became an existentialist again. I've formed an unhealthy obsession with French philosopher and walking trench coat, Albert Camus. The nihilism is freeing, I've found. Once you realise that everything is made up, you can kind of do anything you want (except go on public transport without a mask).
I'm back with my housemates and one of the terrible things I've noticed about living with other students is that you can't ask anyone you live with for advice because nobody has a fucking clue what they're on about. I'm not particularly looking for a piece of advice at the moment but I think it's an observation worth noting.
Drinking is also a thing and I've thought a lot about it. I think there is a correct way to drink, you see. Never drink to get

drunk, you'll only end up vomiting. Never drink to have sex, you'll just end up assaulting someone. Never drink to be confident, your drunk persona is an arsehole.
These are today's thoughts.
I was musing over the words of Shakespeare, 'love all, trust few, do wrong to none', and have decided that this is simply not possible under the current circumstances. My alternative is simple: Love few, ███████ , tolerate the rest.
I am glad you are well and still not dead yet. If you can keep that up until the vaccine comes round, we'll be rolling.

███████████

Creative Writing Society

48 Caterham Street
10th Circle of Hell
YN6 9TP
6th January 2021

26 Dawlish Road
The Abyss
NP4 7YX

Dear ███████,

I think we should run away together. Not now, not tomorrow, but when the pandemic ends. This isn't a demand, it's an invitation. If you leave university and you don't have a clue what you're doing (a state I will surely be in too), come and run away with me.
Let's go to Paris and drink all day like Fitzgerald and Hemingway. Let's go to cafés like Camus and Sartre and sit there until four in the morning just talking about death. Let's go on long walks like Tolkien and Lewis and try and convert the other to our own religions. Let's do it. There's no time to lose. All those people are dead but us – we're living. Wouldn't it be radical? We'll drink excessively, ponder unnecessarily, and swan around in fucking trench coats.
This idea is not compulsory but it is, undeniably, a glorious dream. Perhaps a long weekend, perhaps a few weeks. You have just over a year to agonise and make up excuses. Consider this the cheque you must decide whether to cash in.
I sincerely believe that this declaration is what letters were made for.
Yours,
███████

Liz Lane

A Vaccine for Father Christmas

The Prime Minister was dreaming. For days, something – he couldn't pin down what – had been preying on his mind. In sleep, it finally came to him:
The emerald seating, the gleaming balcony of the House of Commons came into focus. PMQ's had been focused on one issue in particular.
"This is a nightmare", said one Member.
"A catastrophe," muttered another.
The Commons was silent for a moment – a rare instance indeed – as they all brooded.
"Gifts," said one, finally, "are not essential, therefore gift-giving is not an essential service. Moreover," they continued, "nobody knows where to find him. I pose a question to the House: how can you vaccinate someone you can't find?"
A great number of angry shouts filled the House, Members rising to their feet and shaking their fists. Spit, breadcrumbs, and – from the lips of one asymptomatic Member – covid-19 flew through the air.
For a moment, the speaker, too, was incensed, but after a moment he collected himself and bellowed, "ORDER, ORDER."
Another Member rose to their feet, and proclaimed, "Mr Speaker, I wish to tell the Honourable Member in question that they are deluded. We can, quite simply, advertise."
Some scoffed, one mumbled, "that isn't a bad idea, you know."
The Prime Minister, happily, rose to his feet, deciding aloud, "We will advertise! Find Father Christmas!"
Asleep in bed, he let loose a contented snore.
Clapping filled the House. Even an infamous Member, said not to have smiled since the Falklands War, grinned toothily.
The Prime Minister awoke from his slumber full of purpose. I won't tell anyone beforehand, he thought, it'll be spectacular. I'll go up in the polls. They'll love me. I'll be... I'll be... but he couldn't think, his brain had contorted itself into a smile.

The PM was wrapping up his broadcast, "So, if you're out there,

Father Christmas, your vaccine is waiting for you, just register at any NHS mass vaccination site. And as for the rest of you – Stay Alert! Control the Virus! Save Lives!" The broadcast cut out. The PM turned his smug smile onto those behind the camera, and waited for the praise to flood in.

In Cheshire, an old man had just turned off the television. It felt stale, the room felt stale, the air in his lungs no better than rancid.
He thought, as he did every day, I can't do it anymore. But he did. He carried on – not living, that was certain – but just existing.
Yesterday, his son had held up the old man's new granddaughter from the safety of their car, whilst he'd stood by the door and tried to smile. The old man's cataracts were so bad he could only distinguish a small blob and a larger blob in a smudgy car shape. Last night, his son had asked, "Dad, have they contacted you about a vaccine yet?"
"No." The old man was only seventy, he hadn't been to the hospital in years. Others would need it before him. I'm so lonely, he wanted to cry down the phone.
As he thought about the Prime Minister's broadcast, an idea struck him, and it wouldn't let go. He was desperate, it wouldn't let go.

"What do you mean it wasn't Father Christmas putting everything under the tree?" the PM spluttered, loosening his collar, "The housekeeper? I can't believe this."
Since the broadcast, Downing Street had become a hive of activity. "Surely," one civil servant could be overheard saying to his companion, "nobody will take him seriously."

The old man made his way to the hospital. At reception he insisted, "It's me. I'm Father Christmas. I'm here for my vaccination."
A tired-faced receptionist looked him up and down over the

counter. "Tough luck," she smiled ruefully, "you're the fifth we've had in today. You'll just have to wait your turn, I'm afraid."
The old man did his best to return her smile. Deep down he'd known it would never work. As he stepped outside, he began to cry. Sinking down onto a bench, the grey sky seemed to lock him into a cell. For the first time, he said it aloud, although there was nobody near enough to listen, "I can't do it anymore. I can't." As he heard the roar of the underpass, he imagined with eerie clarity just standing up and walking into the traffic.

The old man's son was flipping between two channels on the television. On one, a nurse was being interviewed: "We've got sixty bearded men coming in every day claiming to be Father Christmas, begging for a vaccine. A receptionist in Hertfordshire was mowed down the other day by a group of elderly men." On another, the PM was blaming pensioners who hadn't seen their families in almost a year. Words like 'mob-mentality' seemed to hang in the air before the television, phrases beginning "if people don't follow the rules", and narrowing in on "these individuals."
"Mob mentality," frowned the son. "That doesn't seem right." Back on the former channel, on one half of a split screen, in between sobs a pensioner was apologising, "I don't' (sob), 'I'm so sorry (sob)." He was so spindly, and weeping so violently, it seemed as though his skeleton might be jolted out of his body at any moment.
"The thing is," on the other side of the screen, a small line of text introduced a woman as his daughter, "my dad is getting older, we haven't hugged him since March, and we miss him." They'd muted the microphone of the crying man, but that way, through the television, it seemed like he was screaming.

Madeline Donnelly

Mama Meant Well

Her breath stank of caramelised toffee, no longer oozing, but instead black like the soot on a non stick frying pan. She'd smile. I hated her smile.

I hated the smell of it. That toxic shower of grim drizzle. Then she'd blow a kiss at the door, "night, honey", harassing the brilliant ease of the night, like a shovel pushing through gravel.

Silence followed. Sticky silence. The kind of silence that moaned. I'd wipe my chin hairs with the flat surface of my thumb. Those poor hairs, like dewy weeds on an uneven lawn.

She'd phone every evening before dinner. Twice. But I'd never pick up. I'd let the phone ring out.

And then I'd boil the kettle. Pour the boiled water into the mug with the chipped handle. Open the fridge door. Grab the milk that was curdling at the surface. Curl my eyes at the empty shelves. Forget she phoned.

I'd get dressed in the tracksuit mom gave me last Christmas. Or the Christmas before that. And I'd look for the green socks dad bought me before it happened. Days before it happened. I'd feel a tear of vapour lengthen from a tiny projection of hair on my chin. Longer and longer. Like honey from a dipper.

Then I'd swipe it with the flat surface of my thumb. They're long gone, those socks. I lost them many years ago. I threw them into the stiff warmth of the air, closing my eyes. Dreamt of riding a camel in the desert, far, far away. And I'd watch the sand on the dunes sift through a subtle breeze, a silent, majestic slowness.

Today, her lips were dry. The glass was moist with the condensation of her burnt toffee, the kind I hated. I couldn't smell it. I could only imagine that it stuck in the air, maneuvering through the dry loneliness of the front room. I felt a breeze slap the back of my neck, a sharp drizzle of sleet tickle my wrists. A hollow voice like pushing a shovel through gravel " night, honey".

The corners of my lips turned towards the sky, a whiteness stained yellow. That shovel cleared the streets. It was below freezing.

But that shovel was oozing hot.

Sam Gordon-Webb

An Email

I hope this email finds you well
In these strange and uncertain times
Is an unusual refrain to read
Most days:
What exactly do they mean by
Strange and uncertain?
We all know what's going on
And it sure is strange
That the gym I started going to
To get over a highschool ex
Suddenly would like to let me know
What their coronavirus policy is.

I hadn't much planned on going.

Silas Hand

On the Line

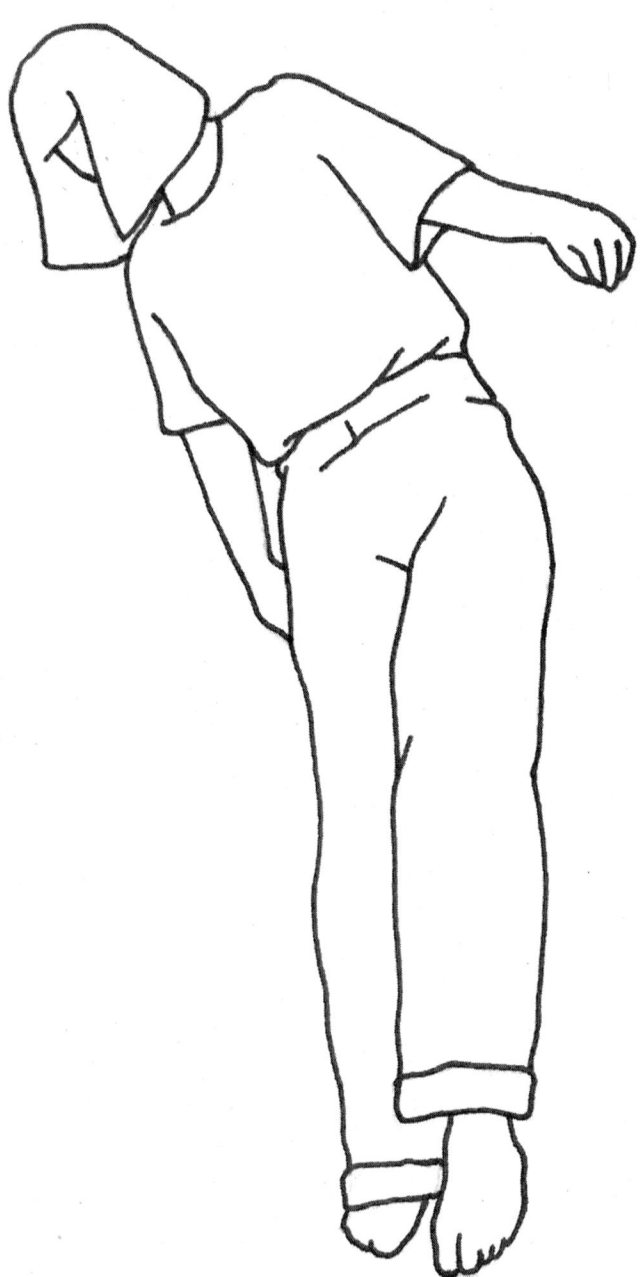

Chapter 4

The Knight

My mind is like a toilet
Grim, overflowing,
Cracked and full of shit

I'm a mass of flesh
Existing whether I like
It or not. I'm here

Mine own stupid head
Doth wander in fantasy
Refuting real life

Oh valiant Sir
Of dazzling wit, huge meat
Why do you cry so?

Clem Hailes

Creative Writing Society

Content Warning

Krishna At Auschwitz	Reference to Holocaust
I Want	Reference to drugs and abuse
Generation Y	Death, suicide, islamophobia. rape, racism, transphobia, homophobia, ableism
Robin	Drugs, overdose, death
Let Me Go	Post-natal depression, suicide
Ghost	Mental health
Ten Easy Steps to Build Confidence	references to eating disroder

Creative Writing Society

Krishna at Auschwitz

Your naked feet make marks in sleet
Where, long ago, the doomed trudged into death.

Immense jaws open wide, swallowing You
Into the entrance of some icy necropolis

Buried beneath snow, a memorial that
Greets You with mottos of human evil –

"Arbeit macht frei."
"Work sets you free."

Dismally You walk on, sluggish memories creeping into You
Of gas chambers guzzling out

All your suffering little children,
As if a flesh factory,

Strangling innumerable souls,
While Nazis, adorned in

Swastikas – symbols the Aryans stole from You –
Laugh like Asuras eating mortals alive.

Images begin to flood Your enlightened mind;
Of corpse clothes dressed in orphaned shoes;

Of mystics, myriad in number, flayed by brutish conquerors;
Of bullets sleeping in babies' bodies, nursing unmarked graves;

Of bloody arrows littering Kauravas' skulls;
Of tanks crushing synagogues;

Of holy lands consumed by nuclear sunlight.

You, O infinite and almighty Lord of Love,
O secret Self hidden in every Soul,

Bear witness to Your Self in all these human reminiscences,
Perverted from Love into Death, Destroyer of Worlds.

At the end of the chambers, at the bottom of this world,
You arrive at the final conclusion of this human horror-show.

An immortal message lies scrawled, wearily,
In frozen stone, carved in every conceivable tongue for all to hear:

"Forever let this place
Be a cry of despair

And a warning to humanity."[1]

Fascism, enveloping the world like the serpent Vritra,
Has brought about this spiritual drought

And delivered too much suffering for
Any Heart of Hearts to bear –

Tears roll down Your azure cheeks,
Merging with winter ice below.

Water joins water.

Atman joins Brahman.

Flowers blossom amidst these vile cemeteries.
Here, within the heart of Death, life begins to bloom anew.

---

[1] Inscription on Auschwitz-Birkenau memorial.

You freeze, meditating for a moment on these dark ages,
On finding just a second of beauty and peace

Buried beneath all this suffering.

Alex Grenfell

I Want

i want to write about big feelings, pink, red and yellow
    about how big and fat and bulging my heart feels
    about pillows round and bursting swimming with
    feathers at the seams
    about the sea and all the huge vast blue green
    underwater hills and peaks and valleys.

i want to write a book, all those thoughts and words and pictures
and voices pinned down neatly like a deer by a spear,
        dripping
i want to write about   myself, about 'i'
    but it feels too thick and black and bold and i
    can't go near it somehow

        about my body, my thick red crusted fingertips and
        shedding eyelashes and the bruises all up and down my
        legs
        about the leaf outside a bedroom window,   veiny and
        green and translucent in the white sun,   tapping tap tap
        against the   smeary glass
        about the people i love, put it down on paper, that
        warm shining feeling that makes me shake and shudder
        and bite at my nails and swallow pill after pill before i
        pass out on the sofa spread

i want to write about everything but i know i never will.

i want to write about absolutely nothing at all, and then i want
to put my pen down forever and climb out of the tiny square of
glass in the attic and slide off the roof into the patch of sunflowers and stinging nettles

i want to write about you and us and i and all that with all the
images and flowers and water and book pages and breakfast
cereals and have it all make sense and plonk itself neatly in a

pattern on the page so people look at it and say look at that beautiful writing, nothing bad could ever be contained or held or put in or extracted from inside it

Eleanor Burleigh

Generation Y

Things that are ok:
Allowing a woman to die as her baby edges out and slips to the floor
A child stepping off the stool as their grades step down
A husband ignoring his wife's no
A muslim woman crying as her headscarf is ripped off
An unwanted baby rotting in a crib
An orangutan plummeting from a tree
A white man crossing the street as a middle eastern man approaches

To our world, a man with a beard
is not a man with a beard.
A vocal threat, the beard contains
secrets that we must fear;
lies, knives, bombs.
The stray hair sticking out
is a fuse to white skin
as the middle-class watch
with their trembling Waitrose carrier bags
flapping from the breeze of uneasy mumbles.
The Waitrose bags make it home, unharmed
and cumin, cloves, cinnamon
and cardamom
tumble out of them
into the hands of
mumblers who are still mumbling:
Such men with such beards
should not be allowed
in a place such as this.

Things that are not ok:
A black man crossing the road
A woman holding her girlfriend's hand
A tube of lipstick a boy has elegantly applied to his lips

On the Line

A lady using her gender's toilet
A woman walking to a place that will unmake her motherhood
A person holding a sign stating that they have the right to be a person
A wheelchair user wanting to be something other than
a sob story or a basketball player.

Think of the children! these pale lips cry
meanwhile upstairs
Timothy watches as his own life pours from his wrist.
Think of the children! they cry,
pumping young minds full of
diazepam, alprazolam, lorazepam
to ease the swelling of the problems
caused by themselves,
their greed, selfishness and sensitivity.
Their enamel groans at every mask ripped off,
every black man shot, every woman's lie.
And they are expected to have the answers,

They are Generation Y.

Ellen Newall

Robin

A robin lay motionless in red leaves. I stared at it from four feet above. At ten, I was considered small for my age. I felt your presence approaching. At seventeen, you seemed huge.
"That's sad," I said, "it's dead."
Mom would have told me it was sleeping.
"Yup," your shadow nodded, "but it's not sad."
I looked up at you for the first time, "Why isn't it sad?"
"Dying is only sad for the people still alive. That bird was probably happy out, eating worms and shit,"
I looked at it again, searching for some trace of happiness in the tiny body.
Then I felt the force of your hands on my shoulder-blades, shoving me head-first into the rotting leaves. Your laugh vibrated from every direction.
I stayed on the ground, my eyes squeezed shut, until the sound of your muddy Nike's crunching on leaves and twigs faded.
When I opened my eyes, the robin was directly in front of me. Freaked out by the maggots feasting on the still beautiful bird, I ran after you, back home.
***
I couldn't guess why you'd brought me along. I took it as a mark of respect.
You and your friends were drinking in the woods under a star-clustered sky. The cruel December air made your hands useless and numb as you fumbled with a lighter for your Benson & Hedges.
"Smoking a fag, when it's freezing cold, looking up at the stars. That makes you feel so fucking alive. The taste of it, the smoke spiralling down into your lungs and back out. That's the best fucking thing," you said, smiling. Your eyes flashed across me for a second.
I stood against a tree, trying to blend into the forest – I didn't want to do the wrong thing, but I wanted to stay with you. I listened while you talked about things I didn't understand, using words I wasn't meant to hear.

I wished the cold would preserve you in ice so you would be like that forever; grinning with your cigarette. I looked up at the sky; the naked trees formed cracks between the stars, the universe like pieces of broken glass.

***

In May, dead leaves from autumn were reborn as bluebells.
You and your friends went to the forest again. This time I wasn't invited.
That was the night you OD'd. You took three yokes to prove you were a man, not a lightweight.
At 6, one of your friends came to the door. His eyes were black holes, his long hair tangled into a nest. The words fell from his mouth like scrabble pieces.
Mom knelt over your body, cradled in the lilac blue blanket. The warm morning sun glowed through the foliage.
People kept talking about the tragedy of it all. Refusing to cry, I kept one picture in my mind: you, your dirty Nike's crushing bluebells, a Benson in your shivering hand, smiling at a broken sky.

Eve O'Donoghue

Let Me Go

I'm meant to be happy. Aren't I? She's in with the nurses now. Behind those grey double doors while I lie here, alone at last. They're "giving me some time to myself." So nice of them. Being alone is the last thing I want right now. See, people always think you need time alone to work through things like this. They leave you for a while if something's wrong; they shut up and think they're doing the right thing. It's not the right thing for me. You're leaving me alone with my thoughts. And that's the worst thing because my head is so wrong right now. It's throbbing, and filled with intrusive thoughts, and it's tearing my mind apart. Less anxiety now and darker thoughts. Hurting myself, or her. Someone. My mind is crumbling and I want to make my body crumble along with it. Simultaneous. I need it to end, but still, here I am, alone.

I turn onto my side in the hospital bed.

They never listen. Nurses. Midwives. I don't think anyone listens. It's a job. A function, not an important part of their lives. I'm not important. I'm a number, a bank account, my details tattooed to my head and when they're done with me - they'll try to make it fast - I'll fade away into the grey mess of people like me. Mothers. People who used their services, and who don't matter anymore. People who paid for their new iPhone. People who paid for their deposit to get a mortgage, but what about my mortgage? My life is my house. I don't want this house anymore, but I'm still paying for other people's. I don't want to live yet here I am, giving life to another being. And to all the midwives. Paying for their lives when I don't know if I want to live mine anymore.

I stare at the leaflet in my hand.

They don't know what to do when they're faced with people like me. Maybe a patronising or inspiring quote, like one they tell all those other mothers. That it's natural at first, or that it'll all fall into place when I take her home, perhaps. They haven't been trained for this, believe me. When I tell them I don't want to hold the baby, as I close my eyes, tears sting, not wanting to look at my own child, the strange entity that has drawn the life from me for the past nine months, they do not know what to say. Because my eyes were closed, I couldn't see their expressions. Probably for the best. But I can imagine. A subtle horror, confusion, perhaps awkwardness at not knowing how to react. I guess I'm a difficult case.

Rare, you know, I said. I'm supposed to be happy. See my smile? Cheshire cat. Grin, smile. What more do you want me to do? I'm a performing monkey for you, aren't I? All of you. Go on, tell me what you want me to do now. Give me actions. Expressions. How am I supposed to feel? Happy? Fine. Smile. Congratulations on the baby, she's beautiful - thanks, thank you so much. She's making me so happy, I can't wait to take her home. She's beautiful, she looks just like me and Billy, she's the perfect child, blonde haired and blue eyed, so perfect, I should take her in my arms, I will -- but I don't want her, don't want her, can't look at her, not a mother, just a woman, girl, stop-- Stop. I don't want to do it anymore. I can't. I can't pretend. Happy, sad, happy, sad, like a switch, I can't switch anymore, it's broken, it doesn't work. I don't work anymore. I used to be a performer. An actress, to everyone, all happy and smiley and now, now that she's finally out, she's broken me in pieces. Ripped me, she's killing me. I'm killing me.

I close my eyes.

She started a while ago, when she was growing inside of me. She started easy, a cruel sense of security, only small kicks and butterflies against my stomach, gentle, and for a moment, I almost enjoyed the idea of having her moving around inside there. Then the kicks got worse. Harder. She started really hurting me. Especially in my stomach, and I'd have the worst sickness, every morning, and it just got worse and worse. It felt like she was rotting my insides, and somehow, I wished she'd rot with it. Like a seed inside of a fruit, I wished she'd go mouldy and I wished she wouldn't come out, not out of me, I wasn't the right fruit. I was a flower. Not a fruit, I didn't need anything inside of me, growing there. She needed a proper mother, a proper womb

to grow inside of, someone who wanted her, I always thought; she needed an apple, a mango tree she could grow on, something able to nourish and nurture her more than I could. I wanted all my nutrition and nourishing to go to myself. And I still do. My body had been taken from me by this little helpless thing inside of me, and every day I resented it more. I was not born to be this fruit. This nourisher, nurturer, this thing willing to let another being live inside of it. I was not born to feel happy about these developments in my life; I was born to feel anxious, and to want it out of my life, out of my world, myself.
I want to be gone.
Let me go.

Lilwen-Meyer Dinkgrafe

Ghost

when you leave
                         i will trace
     ~~trace~~   the ~~paths~~ paths
you made

                                    (with lilting
                                    fingertips,
                                    and song)

rub in
 my ink
 to your etchings,

                             attempt ~~to capture~~
                                    ~~to feel~~
                                    to know

how it was ~~t~~
        that you made
                such art

    without ever committing to
                           paper

Meg Watts

Ten Easy Steps to Build Confidence

Eat the food you want to eat. Allow yourself to indulge in the calories; you need them to survive.

Exercise every day for at least two hours.

Squeeze into a bikini that would have fit you last year. Do not ask for a size up in the dressing room. Buy it anyway. Never take it out of the bag. You will wear it when you deserve it.

Repeat after me: *I am beautiful. I am strong. I am loved.*

Compliment others. Be genuine about it.

Go to the hairdresser. Try something new. Do not get a fringe. It will not suit your bone structure.

Shove fistfuls of sugar in your mouth. Feel the grains grind between your teeth. Feel them turn to sand. Feel the grit on your taste buds.

Do a face mask.

Write a list of things you like about yourself. It can be seemingly insignificant, like the curve of your fingers, or the arch of your brow. Wait a few days. Find something new you admire. Add to this list.

Listen to the advice of strangers online. We are happier than you are.

Rose Ramsden

The University of East Anglia's
Creative Writing Society

Committee 2020–2021

President:	Silas Hand
Vice-President:	Erin Ketteridge
Secretary:	Clara Ehlers
Treasurer:	Alex Eaglestone
Social Secretary:	Mackenzie Malcolm
Health & Safety Officer:	Elif Soyler
Equality & Diversity Officer:	Biff Pearson
Union Council Representative:	Alex Grenfell

With special thanks to Nathan Hamilton of the UEA Publishing Project and Emma Seager of Egg Box Publishing.
Illustrations by Liz Lane.
Cover design by Meg Watts.
Typesetting by Mackenzie Malcolm.

FIN